let's cook

fish & seafood

Carol
Tennant

p

Contents

Calamari

The batter may not be traditional, but this is a perfect dish to serve as part of a selection of tapas, or little dishes, with drinks as they do in Spain.

Serves 4

INGREDIENTS

115 g/4 oz/1 cup plain (all purpose) flour
1 tsp salt
2 eggs

175 ml/6 fl oz/³/₄ cup soda water
450 g/1 lb prepared squid (see method), cut into rings
vegetable oil, for deep-frying

lemon wedges, to serve
parsley sprigs, to garnish

1 Sift the flour into a bowl with the salt. Add the eggs and half the soda water and whisk together until smooth. Gradually whisk in the remaining soda water until the batter is smooth. Set aside.

2 To prepare whole squid, hold the body firmly and grasp the tentacles just inside the body. Pull firmly to remove the innards. Find the transparent 'backbone' and remove. Grasp the wings on the outside of the body and pull to remove the outer skin. Trim the tentacles just below the beak and reserve.

3 Wash the body and tentacles under running water. Slice the body across into 1 cm/½ inch rings. Drain well on paper towels.

4 Meanwhile, fill a deep saucepan about a third full with vegetable oil and heat to 190°F/ 375°F or until a cube of bread browns in 30 seconds.

5 Dip the squid rings and tentacles into the batter, a few at a time, and drop into the hot oil. Fry for 1–2 minutes until crisp and golden. Drain on paper towels. Cook all the squid this way. Serve immediately while still hot with garnished with lemon wedges and parsley.

COOK'S TIP

If you don't like the idea of cleaning squid yourself, get your fishmonger to do it. Sometimes, squid is even sold already cut into rings. Alternatively, you could use prepared baby squid for this dish.

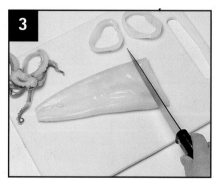

Tempura Whitebait

Tempura is a classic Japanese batter made with egg, flour and water. The batter is very cold and very lumpy, which gives the finished dish its characteristic appearance. It should be eaten straight away.

Serves 4

INGREDIENTS

450 g/1 lb whitebait (smelts),
   thawed if frozen
100 g/3½ oz/¾ cup plain flour
50 g/1¾ oz/⅓ cup cornflour
½ tsp salt
200 ml/7 fl oz /1 cup cold water

1 egg
a few ice cubes
vegetable oil, for deep-frying

CHILLI AND LIME MAYONNAISE:
1 egg yolk

1 tbsp lime juice
1 fresh red chilli, deseeded and finely
   chopped
2 tbsp chopped fresh coriander
200 ml/7 fl oz/1 cup light olive oil
salt and pepper

1 To make the mayonnaise, in the bowl of a food processor or blender, mix together the egg yolk, lime juice, chilli, coriander and seasoning until foaming. With the machine running, gradually add the olive oil, drop by drop to begin with, until the mixture begins to thicken. Continue adding the oil in a steady stream. Adjust seasoning and add a little hot water if the mixture seems too thick. Put to one side.

2 For the tempura whitebait, wash and dry the fish. Set aside on paper towels. In a large bowl, sift together the plain flour, cornflour and salt. Whisk together the water, egg and ice cubes and pour on to the flour. Whisk briefly until the mixture is runny, but still lumpy with dry bits of flour still apparent.

3 Meanwhile, fill a deep saucepan about a third full with vegetable oil and heat to 190°F/ 375°F or until a cube of bread browns in 30 seconds.

4 Dip the whitebait, a few at a time, into the batter and carefully drop into the hot oil. Fry for 1 minute until the batter is crisp but not browned. Drain on paper towels. Cook all the whitebait this way. Serve hot with the chilli and lime mayonnaise.

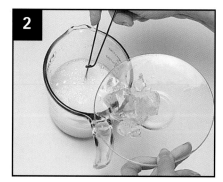

Caesar Salad

Caesar salad was the invention of a chef at a large hotel in Acapulco, Mexico.
It has rightly earned an international reputation.

Serves 4

INGREDIENTS

1 large cos (romaine) lettuce or
  2 hearts of romaine
4 anchovies, drained and halved
  lengthways
Parmesan shavings, to garnish

DRESSING:
2 garlic cloves, crushed

1½ tsp Dijon mustard
1 tsp Worcestershire sauce
4 anchovies in olive oil, drained and
  chopped
1 egg yolk
1 tbsp lemon juice
150 ml/5 fl oz/⅔ cup olive oil

4 tbsp freshly grated Parmesan
  cheese
salt and pepper

CROÛTONS:
4 thick slices day-old bread
2 tbsp olive oil
1 garlic clove, crushed

1 Make the dressing. In a food processor or blender, put the garlic, mustard, Worcestershire sauce, anchovies, egg yolk, lemon juice and seasoning and blend together for 30 seconds, until foaming. Add the olive oil, drop by drop until the mixture begins to thicken then in a steady stream until all the oil is incorporated. Scrape out of the food processor or blender. Add a little hot water if the dressing is too thick. Stir in the grated Parmesan cheese. Taste for seasoning and set aside in the refrigerator until required.

2 For the croûtons, cut the bread into 1 cm/½ inch cubes. Toss with the oil and garlic in a bowl. Transfer to a baking sheet (cookie sheet) in a single. Bake in a preheated oven at 180°C/350°F/ Gas Mark 4, for 15–20 minutes, stirring occasionally, until the croûtons are browned and crisp.

Remove from the oven and allow to cool. Set aside.

3 Separate the cos (romaine) lettuce or hearts of romaine into individual leaves and wash. Tear into pieces and spin dry in a salad spinner. Alternatively, dry the leaves on clean paper towels (kitchen towels). (Excess moisture will dilute the dressing and make the salad taste watery.) Transfer to a plastic bag and refrigerate until needed.

4 To assemble the salad, put the lettuce pieces into a large serving bowl. Add the dressing and toss thoroughly until all the leaves are coated. Top with the halved anchovies, croûtons and Parmesan shavings. Serve at once while still hot.

Tuna Niçoise Salad

This is a classic version of the French Salade Niçoise.
It is a substantial salad, suitable for a lunch or light summer supper.

Serves 4

INGREDIENTS

4 eggs
450 g/1 lb new potatoes
115 g/4 oz/1 cup dwarf green beans,
   trimmed and halved
2 x 175 g/6 oz tuna steaks
6 tbsp olive oil, plus extra for
   brushing

1 garlic clove, crushed
1½ tsp Dijon mustard
2 tsp lemon juice
2 tbsp chopped fresh basil
2 Little Gem lettuces
200 g/7 oz/1½ cups cherry tomatoes,
   halved

175 g/6 oz/2 cups cucumber, peeled,
   cut in half and sliced
50 g/1¾ oz/½ cup pitted black olives
50 g/1¾ oz can anchovies in oil,
   drained
salt and pepper

1 Bring a small saucepan of water to the boil. Add the eggs and cook for 7–9 minutes from when the water returns to the boil – 7 minutes for a slightly soft centre, 9 minutes for a firm centre. Drain and refresh under cold running water. Set aside

2 Cook the potatoes in boiling salted water for 10–12 minutes until tender. Add the beans 3 minutes before the end of the cooking time. Drain both

vegetables well and refresh under cold water. Drain well.

3 Wash and dry the tuna steaks. Brush with a little olive oil and season. Cook on a preheated ridged grill pan for 2–3 minutes each side, until just tender but still slightly pink in the centre. Set aside to rest.

4 Whisk together the garlic, mustard, lemon juice, basil and seasoning. Whisk in the olive oil.

5 To assemble the salad, break apart the lettuces and tear into large pieces. Divide between individual serving plates. Next add the potatoes and beans, tomatoes, cucumber and olives. Toss lightly together. Shell the eggs and cut into quarters lengthways. Arrange these on top of the salad. Scatter over the anchovies.

6 Flake the tuna steaks and arrange on the salads. Pour over the dressing and serve.

VARIATION

Use 2 x 200 g/7 oz cans of tuna in olive oil, drained and flaked, instead of the fresh tuna.

Grilled Red Mullet

*Try to get small red mullet for this dish. If you can only get larger fish,
serve one to each person and increase the cooking time accordingly.*

Serves 4

INGREDIENTS

1 lemon, thinly sliced
2 garlic cloves, crushed
4 sprigs fresh flat-leaf parsley
4 sprigs fresh thyme
8 leaves fresh sage
2 large shallots, sliced
8 small red mullet, cleaned
8 slices Parma ham (prosciutto)
salt and pepper

SAUTE POTATOES AND SHALLOTS:
4 tbsp olive oil
900 g/2 lb potatoes, diced
8 whole garlic cloves, unpeeled
12 small whole shallots

FOR THE DRESSING:
4 tbsp olive oil
1 tbsp lemon juice
1 tbsp chopped fresh flat-leaf parsley
1 tbsp chopped fresh chives
salt and pepper

1 For the sauté potatoes and shallots, heat the olive oil in a large frying pan (skillet) and add the potatoes, garlic cloves and shallots. Cook gently, stirring regularly, for 12–15 minutes until golden, crisp and tender.

2 Meanwhile, divide the lemon slices, halved if necessary, garlic, parsley, thyme, sage and shallots between the cavities of the fish. Season well. Wrap a slice of Parma ham (prosciutto) around each fish. Secure with a cocktail stick (toothpick).

3 Arrange fish on a grill (broiler) pan and cook under a preheated hot grill (broiler) for 5–6 minutes on each side until tender.

4 To make the dressing, mix together the oil and lemon juice with the finely chopped parsley and chives. Season to taste.

5 Divide the potatoes and shallots between 4 serving plates and top each with the fish. Drizzle around the dressing and serve immediately.

Poached Rainbow Trout

As this is served cold, it makes a lovely summer lunch or supper dish.

Serves 4

INGREDIENTS

4 x 375 g/12 oz rainbow trout, cleaned
700 g/1 lb 9 oz new potatoes
3 spring onions (scallions), finely chopped
1 egg, hard-boiled (hard-cooked) and chopped

COURT-BOUILLON:
850 ml/1½ pints/3¾ cups cold water

850 ml/1½ pints/3¾ cups dry white wine
3 tbsp white wine vinegar
2 large carrots, roughly chopped
1 onion, roughly chopped
2 celery sticks, roughly chopped
2 leeks, roughly chopped
2 garlic cloves, roughly chopped
2 fresh bay leaves
4 sprigs fresh parsley
4 sprigs fresh thyme

6 black peppercorns
1 tsp salt

WATERCRESS MAYONNAISE:
1 egg yolk
1 tsp Dijon mustard
1 tsp white wine vinegar
50 g/2 oz watercress leaves, chopped
225 ml/8 fl oz/1 cup light olive oil
salt and pepper

1 First make the court-bouillon. Place all the ingredients in a large saucepan and bring slowly to the boil. Cover and simmer gently for about 30 minutes. Strain the liquid through a fine sieve into a clean pan. Bring to the boil again and simmer fast, uncovered, for 15–20 minutes until the court-bouillon is reduced to 600 ml/ 1 pint/2½ cups.

2 Place the trout in a large frying pan (skillet). Add the court-bouillon and bring slowly to the boil. Remove from the heat and leave the fish in the poaching liquid to go cold.

3 Meanwhile, make the watercress mayonnaise. Put the egg yolk, mustard, wine vinegar, watercress and seasoning into a food processor or blender and blend for 30 seconds until foaming. Begin adding the olive oil, drop by drop, until the mixture begins to thicken. Continue adding the oil in a slow steady stream until it is all incorporated. Add a little hot water if the mixture seems too thick. Season to taste and set aside.

4 Cook the potatoes in plenty of boiling salted water for 12–15 minutes until soft and tender. Drain well and refresh them under cold running water. Set the potatoes aside until cold.

5 When the potatoes are cold, cut them in half if they are very large, and toss thoroughly with the watercress mayonnaise, finely chopped spring onions (scallions) and hard-boiled (hard-cooked) egg.

6 Carefully lift the fish from the poaching liquid and drain on paper towels. Carefully pull the skin away from each of the trout and serve immediately with the potato salad.

Baked Salmon

This is a wonderful dish to serve as part of a buffet lunch or supper and can be served hot or cold.

Serves 8–10

INGREDIENTS

3 kg/6 lb 8 oz salmon filleted
8 tbsp chopped mixed herbs
2 tbsp green peppercorns in brine, drained
1 tsp finely grated lime rind
6 tbsp dry vermouth or dry white wine
salt and pepper
parsley sprigs, to garnish

RED (BELL) PEPPER RELISH:
120 ml/4 fl oz/½ cup white wine vinegar
300 ml/10 fl oz/¼ cups light olive oil
1–2 tsp chilli sauce, to taste
6 spring onions (scallions), finely sliced
1 orange or red (bell) pepper, deseeded and finely diced
1 tbsp chopped fresh flat-leaf parsley
2 tbsp chopped fresh chives

CAPER AND GHERKIN MAYONNAISE:
350 ml/12 fl oz/1½ cups good quality mayonnaise
3 tbsp chopped capers
3 tbsp finely chopped gherkins
2 tbsp chopped fresh flat-leaf parsley
1 tbsp Dijon mustard

1 Wash and dry the salmon fillets and place one fillet, skin side down, on a large sheet of oiled foil. Mix together the herbs, peppercorns and lime rind and spread over the top. Season well and lay the second fillet on top, skin side up. Drizzle over the vermouth or white wine. Wrap the foil over the salmon, twisting well to make a loose but tightly sealed parcel.

2 Transfer the foil parcel to a large baking sheet (cookie sheet) and bake in a preheated oven at 120/C°250°F/Gas Mark ½, for 1½ hours until tender. Remove from the oven and allow to rest for 20 minutes before serving.

3 Meanwhile, make the red (bell) pepper relish. Whisk together the vinegar, olive oil and chilli sauce to taste. Add the spring onions (scallions), red (bell) pepper, parsley and chives. Season and set aside.

4 To make the caper and gherkin mayonnaise, mix all the ingredients together and set aside.

5 Unwrap the cooked salmon and slice thickly. Arrange the slices on a large serving platter and serve with the red (bell) pepper relish and caper and gherkin mayonnaise. Garnish with fresh parsley sprigs.

Barbecued Monkfish

*Monkfish cooks very well on a barbecue
because it is a firm-fleshed fish.*

Serves 4

INGREDIENTS

4 tbsp olive oil
grated rind of 1 lime
2 tsp Thai fish sauce
2 garlic cloves, crushed

1 tsp grated fresh ginger root
2 tbsp chopped fresh basil
700 g/1 lb 9 oz monkfish fillet,
 cut into chunks

2 limes, each cut into 6 wedges
salt and pepper

1 Mix together the olive oil, lime rind, fish sauce, garlic, ginger and basil. Season and set aside.

2 Wash the dry the fish. Add to the marinade and mix well. Leave to marinate for 2 hours, stirring occasionally.

3 If you are using bamboo skewers, soak them in cold water for 30 minutes. Then, lift the monkfish pieces from the marinade and thread them on to the skewers, alternating with the lime wedges.

4 Transfer the skewers, either to a lit barbecue or to a preheated ridged grill pan. Cook for 5–6 minutes, turning regularly, until the fish is tender. Serve immediately.

VARIATION

You could use any type of white fleshed fish for this recipe but sprinkle the pieces with salt and leave for 2 hours to firm the flesh, before rinsing, drying and then adding to the marinade.

Haddock Goujons

Focaccia is an Italian flat bread made with plenty of olive oil. It may include other flavourings as well, including herbs, sun-dried tomatoes and olives. It is widely available in large supermarkets.

Serves 4

INGREDIENTS

175 g/6 oz herb focaccia bread
700 g/1 lb 9 oz skinless, boneless
   haddock fillet
2–3 tbsp plain (all-purpose) flour
2 eggs, lightly beaten
vegetable oil, for deep-frying
lemon wedges, to serve
parsley sprigs, to garnish

TARTARE SAUCE:
1 egg yolk
1 tsp Dijon mustard
2 tsp white wine vinegar
150 ml/5 fl oz/^{2}/$_3$ cup light olive oil
1 tsp finely chopped green olives
1 tsp finely chopped gherkins
1 tsp finely chopped capers

2 tsp chopped fresh chives
2 tsp chopped fresh parsley
salt and pepper

1 Put the foccacia into the bowl of a food processor and blend to fine crumbs. Set aside. Thinly slice the haddock fillet widthways into fingers. Put the flour, egg and breadcrumbs into separate bowls.

2 Dip the haddock fingers into the flour, then the egg and finally the breadcrumbs to coat. Lay on a plate and refrigerate for 30 minutes. For the tartare sauce, put the egg yolk, mustard, vinegar and seasoning into the bowl of a clean food processor. Blend for 30 seconds until frothy. Begin adding the olive oil, drop by drop, until the mixture begins to thicken. Continue adding the olive oil in a slow, steady stream until all the oil is incorporated.

3 Scrape from the food processor bowl into a small mixing bowl and stir in the olives, gherkins, capers, chives and parsley. Check for seasoning. Add a little hot water if the sauce is too thick.

4 Heat a large pan half filled with vegetable oil to 190°C/375°F or until a cube of bread browns in 30 seconds. Cook the haddock goujons, in batches of 3 or 4 for 3–4 minutes until the crumbs are browned and crisp and the fish is cooked. Drain on the kitchen paper and keep warm while you cook the remaining fish.

5 Serve the haddock goujons immediately, with the tartare sauce and lemon wedges.

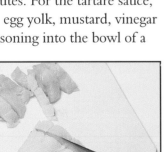

Smoked Fish Pie

What fish cook book would be complete without a fish pie? This is a classic version with smoked fish, prawns (shrimp) and vegetables, in a cheesy sauce, with a more unusual grated potato topping.

Serves 6

INGREDIENTS

2 tbsp olive oil
1 onion, finely chopped
1 leek, thinly sliced
1 carrot, diced
1 celery stick, diced
115 g/4 oz/½ cup button mushrooms, halved if large
grated rind 1 lemon
375 g/12 oz skinless, boneless smoked cod or haddock fillet, cubed

375 g/12 oz skinless, boneless white fish such as haddock, hake or monkfish, cubed
225 g/8 oz cooked peeled prawns (shrimp)
2 tbsp chopped fresh parsley
1 tbsp chopped fresh dill

SAUCE:
50 g/1¾ oz/2 tbsp butter

40 g/1½ oz/⅓ cup plain (all-purpose) flour
1 tsp mustard powder
600 ml/1 pint/2½ cups milk
80 g/3 oz/½ cup Gruyère cheese, grated

TOPPING:
750 g/1½ lb potatoes, unpeeled
50 g/1¾ oz/¼ cup butter, melted
25 g/1 oz Gruyère cheese, grated
salt and pepper

1 For the sauce, heat the butter in a large saucepan and when melted, add the flour and mustard powder. Stir until smooth and cook over a very low heat for 2 minutes without colouring. Slowly beat in the milk until smooth. Simmer gently for 2 minutes then stir in the cheese until smooth. Remove from the heat and put some cling film (plastic wrap) over the surface of the sauce to prevent a skin forming. Set aside.

2 Meanwhile, for the topping, boil the whole potatoes in plenty of salted water for 15 minutes. Drain well and set aside until cool enough to handle.

3 Heat the olive oil in a clean pan and add the onion. Cook for 5 minutes until softened. Add the leek, carrot, celery and mushrooms and cook a further 10 minutes until the vegetables have softened. Stir in the lemon rind and cook briefly.

4 Add the softened vegetables with the fish, prawns (shrimp), parsley and dill to the sauce. Season with salt and pepper and transfer to a greased 1.75 litre/3 pint/7½ cup baking dish.

5 Peel the cooled potatoes and grate coarsely. Mix with the melted butter. Cover the filling with the grated potato and sprinkle with the grated Gruyère cheese.

6 Cover loosely with foil and bake in a preheated oven at 200°C/400°F/Gas Mark 6, for 30 minutes. Remove the foil and bake a further 30 minutes until the topping is tender and golden and the filling is bubbling. Serve immediately with your favourite selection of vegetables.

Tuna Fishcakes

This makes a satisfying and quick mid-week supper.

Serves 4

INGREDIENTS

225 g/8 oz potatoes, cubed
1 tbsp olive oil
1 large shallot, finely chopped
1 garlic clove, finely chopped
1 tsp thyme leaves
2 x 200 g/7 oz cans tuna in olive oil,
  drained
grated rind ½ lemon

1 tbsp chopped fresh parsley
2–3 tbsp plain (all-purpose) flour
1 egg, lightly beaten
115 g/4 oz fresh breadcrumbs
vegetable oil, for shallow frying
salt and pepper

QUICK TOMATO SAUCE:
2 tbsp olive oil
400 g/14 oz can chopped tomatoes
1 garlic clove, crushed
½ tsp sugar
grated rind ½ lemon
1 tbsp chopped fresh basil
salt and pepper

1 For the tuna fishcakes, cook the potatoes in plenty of boiling salted water for 12–15 minutes until tender. Mash, leaving a few lumps, and set aside.

2 Heat the oil in a small frying pan (skillet) and cook the shallot gently for 5 minutes until softened. Add the garlic and thyme leaves and cook for a further minute. Allow to cool slightly then add to the potatoes with the tuna, lemon rind, parsley and seasoning. Mix together well but leave some texture.

3 Form the mixture into 6–8 cakes. Dip the cakes first in the flour, then the egg and finally the breadcrumbs to coat. Refrigerate for 30 minutes.

4 Meanwhile, make the tomato sauce. Put the olive oil, tomatoes, garlic, sugar, lemon rind, basil and seasoning into a saucepan and bring to the boil.

Cover and simmer gently for 30 minutes. Uncover and simmer for a further 15 minutes until thickened.

5 Heat enough oil in a frying pan (skillet) to generously cover the bottom. When hot, add the fishcakes in batches and fry for 3–4 minutes each side until golden and crisp. Drain on paper towels while you fry the remaining fishcakes. Serve hot with the tomato sauce.

Salmon Frittata

A frittata is an Italian slow-cooked omelette, not dissimilar from the Spanish tortilla.
Here it is filled with poached salmon, fresh herbs and vegetables to make a substantial dish.

Serves 6

INGREDIENTS

250 g/9 oz skinless, boneless salmon
3 sprigs fresh thyme
sprig fresh parsley plus 2 tbsp
   chopped fresh parsley
5 black peppercorns
½ small onion, sliced
½ stick celery, sliced
½ carrot, chopped
175 g/6 oz asparagus spears, chopped

80 g/3 oz baby carrots, halved
50 g/1¾ oz/¼ cup butter
1 large onion, finely sliced
1 garlic clove, finely chopped
115 g/4 oz/1 cup peas, fresh or frozen
8 eggs, lightly beaten
1 tbsp chopped fresh dill
salt and pepper
lemon wedges, to garnish

TO SERVE:
crème fraîche
salad
crusty bread

1 Place the salmon in a saucepan with 1 sprig of the thyme, the parsley sprig, peppercorns, onion, celery and carrot. Cover the vegetables and fish with cold water and bring slowly to the boil. Remove the saucepan from the heat and leave to stand for 5 minutes. Lift the fish out of the the poaching liquid, flake the flesh and set aside. Discard the poaching liquid.

2 Bring a large saucepan of salted water to the boil and blanch the asparagus for 2 minutes. Drain and refresh under the cold water. Blanch the carrots for 4 minutes. Drain and refresh under cold water. Drain again and pat dry. Set aside.

3 Heat half the butter in a large frying pan (skillet) and add the onion. Cook gently for 8–10 minutes until softened but not coloured. Add the garlic and remaining sprigs of thyme and cook for a further minute. Add the asparagus, carrots and peas and heat through. Remove from the heat.

4 Add the vegetables to the eggs with the chopped parsley, dill, salmon and seasoning and stir briefly. Heat the remaining butter in the pan and return the mixture to the pan. Cover and cook over a low heat for 10 minutes.

5 Cook under a preheated medium grill (broiler) for a further 5 minutes until set and golden. Serve hot or cold in wedges topped with a dollop of crème fraîche, salad and crusty bread. Garnish with lemon wedges.

Moules Marinières

This dish is much revered in both Belgium and France. Try the chips with a little mayonnaise and enjoy a truly Belgian feast.

Serves 4

INGREDIENTS

900 g/2 lb live mussels
2 shallots, finely chopped
2 garlic cloves, finely chopped
150 ml/5 fl oz/²⁄₃ cup dry
   white wine
2 tbsp chopped fresh parsley
salt and pepper

CHIPS:
900 g/2 lb potatoes
vegetable oil, for deep-frying
salt

TO SERVE (OPTIONAL):
lemon wedges
mayonnaise

1 Clean the mussels by scrubbing or scraping the shells and pulling out any beards. Discard any mussels with broken shells or that refuse to close when tapped sharply.

2 For the chips, cut the potatoes into thin strips, about 1 cm/½ inch thick. Fill a large saucepan or chip pan about one third full of vegetable oil and heat to 140°C/275°F or until a cube of bread browns in 1 minute. Add the chips in 3 batches and cook for 5–6 minutes until the chips are tender but not browned. Drain on paper towels.

3 Put the mussels in a large saucepan with the shallots, garlic and white wine. Cook, covered, over a high heat for 3–4 minutes until all the mussels have opened. Discard any mussels that remain closed. Add the parsley and taste for seasoning. Keep warm while you finish the chips.

4 Increase the temperature of the oil to 190°C/375°F, or until a cube of bread browns in 30 seconds. Cook the chips, again in 3 batches, for 2–3 minutes until golden and crisp. Drain on paper towels and sprinkle with salt.

5 Divide the mussels between 4 large serving bowls. Divide the chips between smaller bowls or plates and serve with lemon wedges and plenty of mayonnaise for dipping chips, if liked.

Seafood Lasagne

A rich dish of layers of pasta, with seafood and mushrooms in a tomato sauce, topped with béchamel sauce and baked until golden.

Serves 6

INGREDIENTS

50 g/1¾ oz/¼ cup butter
40 g/1½ oz/6 tbsp flour
1 tsp mustard powder
600 ml/1 pint/2½ cups milk
2 tbsp olive oil
1 onion, chopped
2 garlic cloves, finely chopped

1 tbsp fresh thyme leaves
450 g/1 lb/3 cups mixed mushrooms, sliced
150 ml/5 fl oz/⅔ cup white wine
400 g/14 oz can chopped tomatoes
450 g/1 lb mixed skinless white fish fillets, cubed

225 g/8 oz fresh scallops, trimmed
4–6 sheets fresh lasagne
225 g/8 oz Mozzarella, drained and chopped
salt and pepper

1 Melt the butter in a saucepan. Add the flour and mustard powder and stir until smooth. Simmer gently for 2 minutes without colouring. Gradually add the milk, whisking until smooth. Bring to the boil and simmer for 2 minutes. Remove from the heat and set aside. Cover the surface of the sauce with cling film (plastic wrap) to prevent a skin forming.

2 Heat the oil in a frying pan (skillet) and add the onion, garlic and thyme. Cook gently for 5 minutes until softened. Add the mushrooms and fry for a further 5 minutes until softened. Stir in the wine and boil rapidly until nearly evaporated. Stir in the tomatoes. Bring to the boil and simmer, covered, for 15 minutes. Season and set aside.

3 Lightly grease a lasagne dish. Spoon half the tomato sauce over the base of the dish and top with half the fish and scallops.

4 Layer half the lasagne over the fish, pour over half the white sauce, add half the Mozzarella. Repeat these layers, finishing with the white sauce and Mozzarella.

5 Bake in a preheated oven at 200°C/400°F/Gas Mark 6 for 35–40 minutes until bubbling and golden and the fish is cooked through. Remove from the oven and leave to stand on a heat resistant surface or mat for 10 minutes before serving.

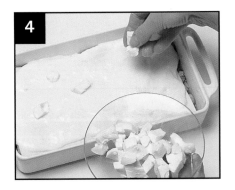

Thai Noodles

*The classic Thai noodle dish, is flavoured with fish sauce,
roasted peanuts and prawns.*

Serves 4

INGREDIENTS

350 g/12 oz cooked, peeled tiger
   prawns (jumbo shrimp)
115 g/4 oz flat rice noodles or rice
   vermicelli
4 tbsp vegetable oil
2 garlic cloves, finely chopped

1 egg
2 tbsp lemon juice
1½ tbsp Thai fish sauce
½ tsp sugar
2 tbsp chopped, roasted peanuts
½ tsp cayenne pepper

2 spring onions (scallions), cut into
   2.5 cm/1 inch pieces
50 g/1¾ oz fresh bean-sprouts
1 tbsp chopped fresh coriander
lemon wedges, to serve

1 Drain the prawns on paper towels to remove excess moisture. Set aside. Cook the rice noodles according to the packet instructions. Drain well and set aside.

2 Heat the oil in a wok or large frying pan (skillet) and add the garlic. Fry until just golden. Add the egg and stir quickly to break it up. Cook for a few seconds.

3 Add the prawns (shrimp) and noodles, scraping down the sides of the pan to ensure they mix with the egg and garlic.

4 Add the lemon juice, fish sauce, sugar, half the peanuts, cayenne pepper, the spring onions (scallions) and half the bean-sprouts stirring quickly all the time. Cook over a high heat for a further 2 minutes until everything is heated through.

5 Turn on to a serving plate. Top with the remaining peanuts and bean-sprouts and sprinkle with the coriander. Serve with lemon wedges.

VARIATION

This is a basic dish to which lots of different cooked seafood could be added. Cooked squid rings, mussels and langoustines would all work just as well.

Jambalaya

Jambalaya is a dish of Cajun origin. There are as many versions of this dish as there are people who cook it. Here is a straightforward one, using prawns (shrimp), chicken and smoked sausage.

Serves 4

INGREDIENTS

2 tbsp vegetable oil
2 onions, roughly chopped
1 green (bell) pepper, deseeded and roughly chopped
2 celery sticks, roughly chopped
3 garlic cloves, finely chopped
2 tsp paprika
300 g/10½ oz skinless, boneless chicken breasts, chopped

100 g/3½ oz kabanos sausages, chopped
3 tomatoes, skinned and chopped
450 g/1 lb/2 cups long-grain rice
900 ml/1½ pint/3¾ cups hot chicken or fish stock
1 tsp dried oregano
2 fresh bay leaves

12 large prawn tails (jumbo shrimp tails)
4 spring onions (scallions), finely chopped
2 tbsp chopped fresh parsley
salt and pepper
salad, to serve

1 Heat the vegetable oil in a large frying pan (skillet) and add the onions, (bell) pepper, celery and garlic. Cook for 8–10 minutes until all the vegetables have softened. Add the paprika and cook for a further 30 seconds. Add the chicken and sausages and cook for 8–10 minutes until lightly browned. Add the tomatoes and cook for 2–3 minutes until collapsed.

2 Add the rice to the pan and stir well. Pour in the hot stock, oregano and bay leaves and stir well. Cover and simmer for 10 minutes over a very low heat.

3 Add the prawns (shrimp) and stir well. Cover again and cook for a further 6–8 minutes until the rice is tender and the prawns (shrimp) are cooked through.

4 Stir in the spring onions (scallions), parsley and season to taste. Serve immediately.

COOK'S TIP

Jambalaya is a dish which has some basic ingredients – onions, green (bell) peppers, celery, rice and seasonings – to which you can add whatever you have to hand.

Salt Cod Hash

As well as being a simple supper dish,
this would make a delicious addition to a brunch menu.

Serves 4

INGREDIENTS

½ quantity Home-salted Cod
4 eggs
3 tbsp olive oil, plus extra for drizzling
8 rashers rindless smoked streaky
   bacon, chopped

700 g/1 lb 9 oz old potatoes, diced
8 garlic cloves
8 thick slices good-quality white
   bread
2 plum tomatoes, skinned and
   chopped

2 tsp red wine vinegar
2 tbsp chopped fresh parsley plus
   extra to garnish
salt and pepper
lemon wedges, to garnish

1 Soak the prepared cod in cold water for 2 hours. Drain well. Bring a large saucepan of water to the boil and add the fish. Remove from the heat and leave to stand for 10 minutes. Drain the fish on paper towels and flake the flesh. Set aside. Discard the soaking water.

2 Bring a saucepan of water to the boil and add the eggs. Simmer the eggs for 7–9 minutes from when the water returns to the boil – 7 minutes for a slightly soft centre, 9 for a firm centre. Immediately drain then plunge the eggs into cold water to stop them cooking further. When cool enough to handle, shell the eggs and roughly chop. Set aside.

3 Add the plum tomatoes, bacon, fish, vinegar and reserved chopped egg to the potatoes and garlic. Cook for a further 2 minutes.Stir in the parsley and season to taste. Put the toast plates and topped with hash parsley and lemon wedges.

4 Toast the bread on both sides until golden. Drizzle with olive oil and set aside.

5 Heat the oil in a large frying pan and add the bacon. Cook over a medium heat for 4–5 minutes until crisp and brown. Remove with a slotted spoon and drain on paper towel. Add the potatoes to the pan with the garlic and cook over a medium heat for 8–10 minutes until crisp and golden.

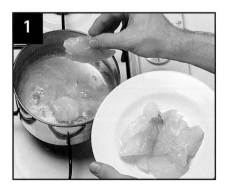

Dover Sole à la Meunière

Dover sole à la Meunière, or 'miller's wife style', gets its name from the light dusting of flour that the fish is given before frying. Seafood chef Rick Stein suggests the addition of a little preserved lemon to give the dish an added piquancy.

Serves 4

INGREDIENTS

50 g/1¾ oz/½ cup plain flour
1 tsp salt
4 x 400 g/14 oz Dover soles, cleaned
  and skinned

150 g/5½ oz/⅔ cup butter
3 tbsp lemon juice
1 tbsp chopped fresh parsley

¼ of a preserved lemon, finely
  chopped (optional)
salt and pepper
lemon wedges, to garnish

1 Mix the flour with the salt and place on a large plate or tray. Drop the fish into the flour, one at a time, and shake well to remove any excess. Melt 40 g/ 1½ oz (3 tablespoons) of the butter in a small saucepan and use to liberally brush the fish all over.

2 Place the fish under a preheated hot grill (broiler) and cook for 5 minutes each side.

3 Meanwhile, melt the remaining butter in pan. Pour cold water into a bowl, large enough to take the base of the pan. Keep nearby.

4 Heat the butter until it turns a golden brown and begins to smell nutty. Remove immediately from the heat and immerse the base of the pan in the cold water, to arrest cooking.

5 Put the fish on to individual serving plates, drizzle with the lemon juice and sprinkle with the parsley and preserved lemon, if using. Pour over the browned butter and serve immediately, garnished with lemon wedges.

COOK'S TIP

If you have a large enough pan (or two) you can fry the floured fish in butter, if you prefer.

Sole Florentine

This is a classic combination of rolled sole fillets in a creamy cheese sauce cooked with spinach. To save time, prepare the cheese sauce in advance.

Serves 4

INGREDIENTS

600 ml/1 pint/2½ cups milk
2 strips lemon rind
2 sprigs fresh tarragon
1 fresh bay leaf
½ onion, sliced
50 g/1¾ oz/2 tbsp butter
50 g/1¾ oz /½ cup plain flour
2 tsp mustard powder

25 g/1 oz/3 tbsp freshly grated
   Parmesan cheese
300 ml/10 fl oz/2¼ cups double
   (heavy) cream
pinch freshly grated nutmeg
450 g/1 lb fresh spinach, washed

4 x 750 g/1 lb 10 oz Dover sole,
   quarter-cut fillets (two from each
   side of the fish)
salt and pepper

TO SERVE:
crisp green salad
crusty bread

1 Put the milk, lemon rind, tarragon, bay leaf and onion into a saucepan and bring slowly to the boil. Remove from the heat and set aside for 30 minutes for the flavours to infuse.

2 Melt the butter in a clean saucepan and stir in the flour and mustard powder until smooth. Strain the infused milk, discarding the lemon, herbs and onion. Gradually beat the milk into the butter and flour until smooth. Bring slowly to the boil, stirring constantly, until thickened. Simmer gently for 2 minutes. Remove from the heat and stir in the cheese, double (heavy) cream, nutmeg and seasoning. Cover the surface of the sauce with baking parchment or cling film (plastic wrap) and set aside.

3 Lightly grease a large baking dish. Blanch the spinach leaves in plenty of boiling salted water for 30 seconds. Drain and immediately refresh under cold water. Drain and pat dry. Put the spinach in a layer on the bottom of the greased dish.

4 Wash and dry the fish fillets. Season and roll up. Arrange on top of the spinach and pour over the cheese sauce. Transfer to a preheated oven at 200°C/400°F/ Gas Mark 6 and cook for 35 minutes until bubbling and golden. Serve immediately with a crisp green salad and crusty bread.

VARIATION

For a budget version of this dish, use lemon sole instead of Dover sole.

Sea Bass with Ratatouille

Sea bass is surely the king of round fish, with a delightful flavour and texture. Here it is cooked very simply and served with a highly flavoured sauce of ratatouille and a basil dressing.

Serves 4

INGREDIENTS

2 large sea bass, filleted
olive oil, for brushing
salt and pepper

RATATOUILLE:
1 large aubergine
2 medium courgettes
1 tbsp sea salt
4 tbsp olive oil

1 medium onion, roughly chopped
2 garlic cloves, crushed
½ red (bell) pepper, deseeded and
   roughly chopped
½ green (bell) pepper, deseeded and
   roughly chopped
2 large ripe tomatoes, skinned and
   chopped
1 tbsp freshly chopped basil

DRESSING:
5 tbsp roughly chopped fresh basil
2 garlic cloves, roughly chopped
4 tbsp olive oil
1 tbsp lemon juice
salt and pepper

1 To make the ratatouille, cut the aubergine (eggplant) and courgette (zucchini) into chunks about the same size as the onion and (bell) peppers. Put the aubergine (eggplant) and courgette (zucchini) in a colander with the salt and set aside to drain for 30 minutes. Rinse thoroughly and pat dry on paper towels. Set aside.

2 Heat the oil in a large saucepan and add the onion and garlic. Cook gently for 10 minutes until softened. Add the (bell) peppers, aubergine (eggplant) and courgette (zucchini). Season and stir well. Cover and simmer very gently for 30 minutes until all the vegetables have softened. Add the tomatoes and cook for a further 15 minutes.

3 Meanwhile make the dressing. Put the basil, garlic, and half the olive oil into a food processor and blend until finely chopped. Add the remaining olive oil, lemon juice and seasoning.

4 Season the sea bass fillets and brush with a little oil. Preheat a frying pan (skillet) until very hot and add the fish, skin side down. Cook for 2–3 minutes until the skin is browned and crispy. Turn the fish and cook for a further 2–3 minutes until just cooked through.

5 To serve, stir the basil into the ratatouille then divide between 4 serving plates. Top with the fresh fried fish and spoon around the dressing.

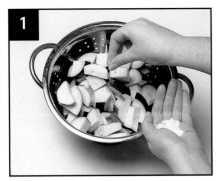

Cold Poached Cod Steaks
with a Pickled Vegetable Relish

Poached cod has a very delicate flavour.
Here it is teamed with a piquant relish of finely diced, colourful vegetables, both served cold

Serves 4

INGREDIENTS

1 small carrot, thinly sliced
1 small onion, thinly sliced
1 celery stick, thinly sliced
3 sprigs fresh parsley
3 sprigs fresh thyme
1 garlic clove, sliced
1.75 litres/3 pints/7½ cups water
1 tsp salt
4 x 175 g/6 oz cod steaks

PICKLED VEGETABLE RELISH:
1 small carrot, finely diced
¼ red (bell) pepper, deseeded and
 finely diced
½ small red onion, finely diced
1 garlic clove, finely chopped
3 tbsp finely diced cornichon pickles
4 tbsp chopped pitted green olives
1 tbsp capers, drained and rinsed

2 salted anchovies, soaked in several
 changes of water for 15 minutes,
 chopped
1 tbsp red wine vinegar
100 ml/3½ fl oz/scant ½ cup
 olive oil
2 tbsp chopped fresh parsley
salt and pepper
salad leaves, to serve

1 Put the carrot, onion, celery, parsley, thyme, garlic, water and salt into a large saucepan. Bring to the boil and simmer gently for 10 minutes. Add the fish and poach for 5–7 minutes until just firm in the centre. Remove the fish with a slotted spoon and leave to cool. Refrigerate for 2 hours.

2 Meanwhile, make the pickled vegetable relish. In a non-metallic bowl, combine the carrot, red (bell) pepper, red onion, garlic, cornichons, olives, capers, anchovies, vinegar, olive oil and parsley. Season to taste, adding a little more vinegar or olive oil to taste. Cover and leave to stand in the refrigerator for 1 hour.

3 To serve, place a cold cod steak on each of 4 serving plates. Spoon the relish over the top. Serve immediately with dressed salad leaves.

Luxury Fish Pie

This is a fish pie for pushing out the boat!

Serves 4

INGREDIENTS

80 g/3 oz/½ cup butter
3 shallots, finely chopped
115 g/4 oz/2 cups button mushrooms, halved
2 tbsp dry white wine
900 g/2 lb live mussels, scrubbed and bearded
1 quantity court-bouillon (see Poached Rainbow Trout, page 14)
300 g/10½ oz monkfish fillet, cubed

300 g/10½ oz skinless cod fillet, cubed
300 g/10½ oz skinless lemon sole fillet, cubed
115 g/4 oz tiger prawns (jumbo shrimp), peeled
25 g/1 oz/¼ cup plain (all purpose) flour
50 ml/2 fl oz/¼ cup double (heavy) cream

POTATO TOPPING:
1.5 kg/3 lb 5oz floury potatoes, cut into chunks
50 g/1¾ oz/¼ cup butter
2 egg yolks
120 ml/4 fl oz/½ cup milk
pinch freshly grated nutmeg
salt and pepper
fresh parsley, to garnish

1 For the filling, melt 25 g/1 oz of the butter in a frying pan (skillet), add the shallots and cook for 5 minutes until softened. Add the mushrooms and cook over a high heat for 2 minutes. Add the wine and simmer until the liquid has evaporated. Transfer to a 1.5 litre/2¾ pint/6¼ cup shallow ovenproof dish and set aside.

2 Put the mussels into a large saucepan with just the water clinging to their shells and cook, covered, over a high heat for 3–4 minutes until all the mussels have opened. Discard any that remain closed. Drain, reserving the cooking liquid. When cool enough to handle, remove the mussels from their shells and add to the mushrooms.

3 Bring the court-bouillon to the boil and add the monkfish. Poach gently for 2 minutes before adding the cod, sole and prawns (shrimp). Poach a further 2 minutes. Remove the fish with a slotted spoon and add to the mussels and mushrooms.

4 Melt the remaining butter in a saucepan and add the flour. Stir until smooth and cook for 2 minutes without colouring.

Gradually, stir in the hot court-bouillon and mussel cooking liquid until smooth and thickened. Add the cream and simmer gently for 15 minutes, stirring. Season to taste and pour over the fish.

5 Meanwhile, make the topping. Boil the potatoes in plenty of salted water for 15–20 minutes until tender. Drain well and mash with the butter, egg yolks, milk, nutmeg and seasoning. Pipe over the fish, or spread with a spatula, and roughen the surface of the topping with a fork.

6 Bake the finished fish pie in a preheated oven at 200°C/400°F/Gas Mark 6, for 30 minutes until golden and bubbling. Serve straight from the oven, piping hot with a garnish of fresh parsley.

This is a Parragon Book
First published in 2003

Parragon
Queen Street House
4 Queen Street, Bath, BA1 1HE, UK

ISBN: 1-40540-823-5

Printed in China

NOTE

This book uses imperial and metric measurements. Follow the same units
of measurement throughout; do not mix imperial and metric. All spoon
measurements are level; teaspoons are assumed to be 5 ml and
tablespoons are assumed to be 15 ml. Unless otherwise stated, milk is
assumed to be whole milk, eggs and individual vegetables such as
potatoes are medium, and pepper is freshly ground black pepper.

The times given for each recipe are an approximate guide only because
the preparation times may differ according to the techniques used by
different people and the cooking times may vary as a result of the type of
oven used.

Recipes using raw or very lightly cooked eggs should be avoided by
infants, the elderly, pregnant women, convalescents and anyone suffering
from an illness.